P9-DDV-557

3 1526 04371197 4

YOU'RE THE CHEF

DELICIOUS Vegetarian MAIN DISHES

Jennifer S. Larson Photographs by **Brie Cohen**

MILLBROOK PRESS • MINNEAPOLIS

For my veggie-loving husband, Michael —J.S.L.

For Jaci, a wonderful cook, foodie, and best friend —B.C.

Photography by Brie Cohen
Food in photographs prepared by chef David Vlach
Illustrations by Laura Westlund/Independent Picture Service
The image on page 5 is used with the permission of © iStockphoto.com/stuartbur.

Allergy alert: The recipes in this book contain ingredients to which some people can be allergic. Anyone with food allergies or sensitivities should follow the advice of a physician or other medical professional.

Copyright © 2013 by Lerner Publishing Group, Inc.

All rights reserved. International copyright secured. No part of this book may be reproduced, stored in a retrieval system, or transmitted in any form or by any means—electronic, mechanical, photocopying, recording, or otherwise—without the prior written permission of Lerner Publishing Group, Inc., except for the inclusion of brief quotations in an acknowledged review.

Millbrook Press
A division of Lerner Publishing Group, Inc.
241 First Avenue North
Minneapolis, MN 55401 U.S.A.

Website address: www.lernerbooks.com

Main body text set in Fellbridge Standard.
Typeface provided by Monotype Typography.

Library of Congress Cataloging-in-Publication Data

Larson, Jennifer S., 1967– author.
Delicious vegetarian main dishes / by Jennifer Larson ; photographs by Brie Cohen.
    pages   cm — (You're the chef)
      Includes index.
   ISBN 978–0–7613–6635–5 (lib. bdg. : alk. paper)
1. Vegetarian cooking—Juvenile literature. 2. Entrees (Cooking)—Juvenile literature.
    I. Cohen, Brie, illustrator. II. Title.
        TX837.L28 2013
641.5'636—dc23   2012020923

Manufactured in the United States of America
1 – BP – 12/31/12

TABLE OF CONTENTS

Are you ready to make some tasty vegetarian food? YOU can be the chef and make food for yourself and your family. These easy recipes are perfect for a chef who is just learning to cook. And they're so delicious, you'll want to make them again and again!

I developed these recipes with the help of my kids, who are seven and ten years old. They can't do all the cooking on their own yet, but they can do a lot.

Can't get enough of cooking? Check out www.lerneresource.com for bonus recipes, healthful eating tips, links to cooking technique videos, metric conversions, and more!

BEFORE YOU START

Reserve your space! Always ask for permission to work in the kitchen.

Find a helper! You will need an adult helper for some tasks. Talk with this person to decide what steps you can do on your own and what steps the adult will help with.

Make a plan! Read through the whole recipe before you start cooking. Do you have the ingredients you'll need? If you don't know what a certain ingredient is, see page 31 to find out more. Do you understand each step? If you don't understand a technique, such as *whisk* or *slice*, turn to page 7. At the beginning of each recipe, you'll see how much time you'll need to prepare the recipe and to cook it. The recipe will also tell you how many servings it makes. Small drawings at the top of each recipe let you know what major kitchen equipment you'll need—such as a stovetop, a blender, or a microwave.

stovetop

blender

knife

microwave

oven

Wash up! Always wash your hands with soap and water before you start cooking. And wash them again after you touch raw eggs, meat, or fish.

Get it together! Find the tools you'll use, such as measuring cups or a mixing bowl. Gather all the ingredients you'll need. That way you won't have to stop to look for things once you start cooking.

SAFETY TIPS

That's sharp! Your adult helper needs to be in the kitchen when you are using a knife, a grater, or a peeler. If you are doing the cutting, use a cutting board. Cut away from your body, and keep your fingers away from the blade.

That's hot! Be sure an adult is in the kitchen if you use the stove or the oven. Your adult helper can help you cook on the stove and take hot things out of the oven.

Tie it back! If you have long hair, tie it back or wear a hat. If you have long sleeves, roll them up. You want to keep your hair and clothing out of the food and away from flames or other heat sources.

Turn that handle! When cooking on the stove, turn the pot handle toward the back. That way, no one will accidentally bump the pot and knock it off the stove.

Wash it! If you are working with raw eggs or meat, you need to keep things extra clean. After cutting raw meat or fish, wash the knife and the cutting board right away. They must be clean before you use them to cut anything else.

Go slowly! Take your time when you're working. When you are doing something for the first time, such as peeling or grating, be sure not to rush.

Above all, have fun!

Finish the job right!

One of your most important jobs as a chef is to clean up when you're done. Wash the dishes with soap and warm water. Wipe off the countertop or the table. Put away any unused ingredients. The adults in your house will be more excited for you to cook next time if you take charge of cleaning up.

COOKING TOOLS

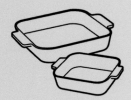 baking pans

 bowls

 can opener

 colander

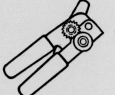 cookie sheet

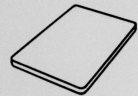 cutting board

dish towel

 dry measuring cups

fork

 frying pan

 grater

knives

large spoon

 liquid measuring cup

measuring spoons

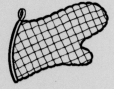 oven mitt

 pie pan

 plate

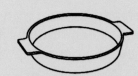 round baking pan

 saucepans

 serrated knife

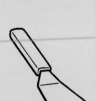 spatula

 vegetable peeler

whisk

 wooden spoon

6

TECHNIQUES

bake: to cook in the oven

boil: to heat liquid on a stovetop until the liquid starts to bubble

chop: to cut food into small pieces using a knife

cover: to put a lid on a pan or pot containing food

discard: to throw away or put in a compost bin. Discarded parts of fruits and vegetables and eggshells can be put in a compost bin, if you have one.

drain: to pour the liquid off a food. You can drain food by pouring it into a colander or strainer. If you are draining water or juice from canned food, you can also use the lid to hold the food back while the liquid pours out.

grate: to use a food grater to shred food into small pieces

grease: to rub butter or oil on a pan or in

muffin tins to prevent food from sticking when it bakes.

mix: to stir food using a spoon or fork

preheat: to turn the oven to the temperature you will need for baking. An oven takes about 15 minutes to heat up.

serrated: a tool, such as a knife, that has a bumpy edge

set aside: to put nearby in a bowl or plate or on a clean work space

simmer: to boil at a low heat setting. The liquid will be boiling with very tiny bubbles.

slice: to cut food into thin pieces

sprinkle: to scatter on top

thaw: to warm up frozen food until it is soft

whisk: to stir quickly with a fork or whisk

MEASURING

To measure **dry ingredients**, such as sugar or flour, spoon the ingredient into a measuring cup until it is full. Then use the back of a table knife to level it off. Do not pack it down unless the recipe tells you to. Do not use measuring cups made for liquids.

When you're measuring a **liquid**, such as milk or water, use a clear glass or plastic measuring cup. Set the cup on the table or a counter and pour the liquid into the cup. Pour slowly and stop when the liquid has reached the correct line.

Don't measure your ingredients over the bowl they will go into. If you accidentally spill, you might have way too much!

serves 6

preparation time: 20 to 25 minutes
baking time: 35 to 40 minutes

ingredients:

1 tablespoon butter
3 slices wheat bread
1 large stalk broccoli
2 cups water
4 ounces shredded cheddar cheese
6 eggs
2 cups milk
1 teaspoon salt
sprinkle of pepper

equipment:

cutting board
knife
paper towel
9 x 13 inch baking pan
liquid measuring cup
medium saucepan
colander
medium bowl
fork or whisk
teaspoons
oven mitts

Eggxtra Tasty Bake

Make this egg bake for a breakfast or brunch—
or even for an eggy dinner.

1. **Preheat** the oven to 350°F. Use a knife and cutting board to **cut** 1 tablespoon of butter. Markings on the butter's wrapping will show you where to cut. Put the butter on a paper towel and use it to **grease** the entire baking pan. Be sure to get the corners.

2. **Tear** the bread into pieces about the size of a quarter. **Lay** the pieces of bread in the pan, covering the whole pan.

3. **Wash** the broccoli in cool water. Use a knife and cutting board to cut the broccoli. **Cut** off the bottom of the broccoli stem and discard. Cut the rest of the stem into large circular chunks. Then cut the broccoli tops lengthwise into several large pieces. Cut enough to make about 2 cups.

4. **Pour** 2 cups of water into a medium saucepan, and put broccoli in the pan. Turn the burner under the pot on high. When the water begins to boil, turn the burner to low. Cook broccoli until just tender, about 5 to 7 minutes. To check if it's done, stick a fork into a piece. The fork should slide in easily.

5. When broccoli is done cooking, have an adult **drain** it into a colander. Run broccoli under cold water. When it is cool, **cut** the tender stem chunks and tops into small pieces.

6. **Put** broccoli into the baking pan on top of bread pieces. **Sprinkle** shredded cheese on top.

7. In a medium bowl, **crack** the eggs. **Whisk** eggs with a fork or whisk until mixed. **Add** milk, salt, and pepper. **Mix** egg mixture with a fork or a whisk. **Pour** over broccoli, bread, and cheese in the pan.

8. Use oven mitts to **place** the pan in the oven. **Bake** for 35 to 40 minutes. Use oven mitts to **remove** the pan from the oven. Serve.

Note:

If you want to have this for breakfast, you can make it the night before. Follow all the steps except baking it. Then cover the pan with plastic wrap or aluminum foil and put it in the refrigerator. In the morning, all you need to do is preheat the oven and bake the dish. It will need an extra 5 minutes in the oven to heat all the way through.

serves 4

preparation time: 20 to 25 minutes
cooking time: 30 seconds

ingredients:

1 cup frozen corn
½ red or green pepper
1 medium tomato
½ lemon
1 tablespoon vegetable oil
1 tablespoon fresh cilantro
   (optional)
1 14-ounce can black beans
pinch of salt
1 to 2 sprinkles of pepper
1 sprinkle of cayenne pepper
   (if you like it a little spicy)

equipment:

small microwave-safe bowl
cutting board
knife
serrated knife
small bowl
spoon
plastic wrap
measuring spoons
can opener
colander
medium bowl

Simple Black Bean Salad

This quick and easy salad tastes good on a hot day.
Or take it to school in your lunch!

1. **Put** frozen corn in microwave-safe bowl and place it in the microwave for 30 seconds. The corn should be thawed, but it does not need to be hot. Set aside.

2. **Wash** the green pepper and tomato under cool water.

3. Use a cutting board and knife to cut the vegetables. To **cut** the green pepper, first cut around stem. Then cut the green pepper in half and remove the seeds. Discard the stem and seeds. **Chop** the rest of the green pepper. Set aside.

4. It works best to cut a tomato with a serrated knife, a knife with bumps along the sharp edge. To cut the tomato, first **cut** out the brown circle on the top. Discard it. Then **chop** the rest of the tomato. Set aside.

5. On the cutting board, **cut** the lemon in half. **Squeeze** ½ lemon into a small bowl to get the juice out. You will need to **scoop** out the seeds with a small spoon. Squeeze enough to make 2 tablespoons. Wrap the other half of the lemon in plastic wrap and save it for another time.

6. Measure 1 tablespoon of vegetable oil. **Add** it to the lemon juice.

7. **Wash** the cilantro under cool water and pat it dry with a towel. To prepare it, **pull** the leaves from the stems. Use a knife and cutting board to **chop** the leaves into small pieces.

8. Use the can opener to **open** the black beans. Put a colander in the sink and **pour** the beans into the colander to drain the liquid.

9. **Put** the green pepper, tomato, lemon juice mixture, cilantro, and beans in a medium bowl. **Sprinkle** in a pinch of salt and pepper. **Add** 1 or 2 sprinkles of cayenne pepper if you like it spicy. **Mix** all the ingredients together with a spoon. Serve.

TRY THIS!
Add some chopped avocado or green onions to this salad.

serves 4 to 6

preparation time: 20 to 25 minutes
cooking time: 25 to 30 minutes

ingredients:

1 carrot
½ green pepper
2 green onions
3 ounces cheddar or Monterey
   Jack cheese
½ cup refried beans
½ cup salsa
3 whole wheat tortillas

equipment:

vegetable peeler
grater
cutting board
knife
measuring cups—¼ cup, ½ cup
can opener
spoon
pie pan or round 9-inch baking
   pan
oven mitts

Tortilla Tower

You'll have fun layering tasty fillings
in this version of a burrito.

1. **Preheat** the oven to 350°F.

2. **Wash** the carrot, the green pepper,
and green onions in cool water.

3. Use the vegetable peeler to
remove the outer skin from
the carrot. **Grate** the carrots
using the grater. Discard the
stem. Set aside grated carrot
and wash the grater.

TRY THIS!

For more yummy flavor,
try adding **black olives**,
mushrooms, or **tomatoes**
to the mix. You can also replace
the salsa with pasta sauce if
you want the recipe
less spicy.

4. Use the cutting board and knife to cut the other vegetables. To cut the green pepper, **cut** around the stem. Then cut the green pepper in half and remove the seeds. Discard the stem and seeds. **Cut** the rest of the pepper in half. Save one half for another time. **Chop** the other half of the green pepper. Set aside.

5. To chop the green onions, **cut** off the roots and discard. Remove any dry or wilted green parts. Then **slice** the onions into small pieces about ½ inch long. You can use both the white and green parts of the onion.

Turn the page for more Tortilla Tower

6. Use the grater to **grate** ¾ cup cheese. Set aside.

7. Use the can opener to **open** the refried beans. Use a spoon and measuring cup to **scoop** out ½ cup.

8. Measure ¼ cup salsa. **Pour** the salsa into a pie pan so that the bottom is lightly covered. Measure another ¼ cup of salsa. Set aside.

9. **Place** 1 tortilla on top of the salsa in the pan.

10. **Spread** half of the measured beans on the tortilla. **Sprinkle** some green pepper, carrots, and green onions on the beans. **Spoon** a little salsa on the toppings. **Sprinkle** with a third of the cheese.

11. **Place** another tortilla on top of the vegetables and cheese, and repeat step 10.

12. **Place** the last tortilla on top. **Sprinkle** with the rest of the cheese.

13. Use oven mitts to **put** the pan in the oven. **Bake** for 25 to 30 minutes, or until the cheese on top is melted and brown. Remove the pan from the oven with oven mitts. Use a knife to **cut** the tortilla tower into slices, like a pie. Serve.

Crispy Tofu Sticks

Serve this tasty tofu dish with rice and a vegetable for dinner. Or have these sticks for an afternoon snack with ketchup.

serves 4

preparation time: 20 minutes
cooking time: 30 to 35 minutes

1. **Preheat** the oven to 375°F.

2. **Cut** open the tofu package. If the tofu is packed in water, **drain** the water into the sink.

ingredients:
12 ounces firm or extra-firm tofu
4 saltine crackers
2 tablespoons whole wheat bread crumbs
1 teaspoon chili powder
¼ teaspoon salt
3 tablespoons vegetable oil
ketchup

3. Use 2 to 3 paper towels or a dish towel to pat the tofu dry. Gently **squeeze** the tofu on all sides with the towel. Don't squeeze too hard, or the tofu might fall apart.

Turn the page for more Crispy Tofu Sticks

equipment:
paper towels or dish towel
knife
cutting board
1 gallon size ziplock plastic bag
2 shallow bowls
measuring spoons
spoon
9 x 13-inch baking pan
spatula
4 plates

Crispy Tofu Sticks continued

4. Use a knife and cutting board to cut the tofu. **Slice** it in pieces about 3 inches long and ½ inch thick.

5. **Place** the crackers in a plastic bag, and seal it shut. Use your hands to **crush** the crackers in the bag. The cracker pieces should be smaller than the size of a pea. **Pour** the crushed crackers into a shallow bowl.

6. Measure the bread crumbs, chili powder, and salt. **Add** them to the crackers and mix with a spoon.

7. Use a measuring spoon to **pour** 1 tablespoon of oil in a baking pan. **Spread** the oil around with a spatula.

8. **Pour** 2 tablespoons of oil in another shallow bowl.

9. Gently take a piece of tofu and **dip** it in the bowl of oil. Make sure the oil coats all sides of the tofu. Then place the tofu in the crumb mixture. **Roll** it gently until it is coated on all sides. Place it in the baking pan. Repeat with the rest of the tofu pieces. The pieces can be close together in the pan, but not touching.

10. Use oven mitts to **put** the pan in the oven. **Bake** for 30 to 35 minutes, until tofu is golden brown and crisp. Take the pan out of the oven.

11. Use a spatula to **place** the tofu pieces on 4 plates. Serve with ketchup for dipping!

TRY THIS!

Dip these tofu treats in soy sauce, ranch dressing, mustard, or anything else you dream up. Experiment!

serves 4

preparation time: 15 minutes
cooking time: 25 to 30 minutes

ingredients:

1 small onion
2 medium potatoes
1 14-ounce can garbanzo beans
2 tablespoons vegetable oil
1 teaspoon mild curry powder
½ teaspoon ground ginger
2 cups water or vegetable broth
1 cup white rice
½ cup frozen peas
½ cup raisins
¼ cup unsalted cashews
½ teaspoon salt

equipment:

knife
cutting board
measuring cups—¼ cup,
  ½ cup, 1 cup
can opener
colander
measuring spoons
large saucepan with lid
liquid measuring cup

Curried Potatoes and Rice

Impress your family with this delicious and
healthy vegetable and rice dish.

1. Use a knife and a cutting board to **cut** off
both ends of the onion. Set the onion on
one of the flat parts you made by cutting it.
Cut the onion in half. **Peel** off and discard
the papery layers around the outside.
Lay the onion half flat on the
cutting board. **Cut** the
onion crosswise into
semicircular slices.
Then **chop** the slices into
small pieces. Repeat with
the other half. Set aside.

2. **Wash** the potatoes in
cool water. Use a cutting
board and knife to cut the
potatoes. First, **slice**
a potato into 1/2-inch
circles. Then **chop** each
slice into 1/2-inch pieces.
Cut enough to make 1 cup.

3. Use a can opener to **open** the can of beans. Put a colander in the sink and **pour** the beans into the colander to drain the liquid.

4. Use a measuring spoon to **pour** 2 tablespoons of oil in a large saucepan. Turn the burner under the pot to medium. **Add** the onion and cook for 5 minutes. **Add** the potato and cook for 6 to 8 minutes.

5. Use measuring spoons to **add** the mild curry powder and ginger. Cook for 1 to 2 minutes.

6. **Add** water or vegetable broth and rice to the saucepan. **Cover** and cook on high until it is boiling. Turn to low heat. Cook for 15 to 17 minutes, until rice is cooked. To check if the rice is done, use a spoon to **scoop** some out. Let the rice cool and then taste it to see if it is tender. If not, let it cook for a few more minutes.

7. **Add** beans, peas, raisins, and cashews to the saucepan. **Stir** for 3 to 5 minutes until heated through.

8. **Stir** in salt and serve.

serves 4

preparation time: 15 to 20 minutes
cooking time: 10 minutes

ingredients:

1 14-ounce can pinto beans
3 to 4 green onions
1 medium tomato
4 ounces cheddar cheese
½ cup salsa
4 medium baking potatoes

equipment:

can opener
knife
cutting board
5 small bowls
serrated knife
grater
measuring cups—1 cup, ½ cup
fork
4 paper towels
microwave-safe plate
5 spoons
4 dinner plates

Baked Potato Pileup

This baked potato is a meal all by itself. Pile your potato with your favorite toppings.

1. Use a can opener to **open** the beans. Put a colander in the sink, and **pour** the beans into the colander to drain the liquid. Put the beans in a small bowl.

2. **Wash** the green onions and the tomato in cool water.

3. Use a knife and a cutting board to cut the vegetables. To chop the green onion, **cut** off the roots and discard. Remove any dry or wilted green parts. Then **slice** the onions into small pieces about ½-inch long. You can use both the white and green parts of the onion. Put the onions in a small bowl.

4. It works best to cut a tomato with a serrated knife, a knife with bumps along the sharp edge. To cut the tomato, first **cut** out the brown circle on the top. **Discard** it. Then **chop** the rest of the tomato. Put the chopped tomato in a small bowl.

5. Use a grater to **grate** 1 cup of cheese. Place cheese in a small bowl.

6. **Measure** ½ cup of salsa into a small bowl.

Turn the page for more Baked Potato Pileup

Note:
Did you know that the skin is one of the healthiest parts of a potato? You can eat it too!

Baked Potato Pileup continued

7. **Wash** the potatoes well under warm water. Use a fork to **poke** holes in each potato in 4 or 5 different places. Run a little water on 4 paper towels to get them damp. They should not be sopping wet. Wrap each potato in a damp paper towel.

8. **Place** the potatoes on a microwave-safe plate. Put the plate in the microwave. Cook on high for 8 minutes. To check if they are done, **poke** a potato with a fork. If the fork goes in easily, they are ready. If not, cook them in the microwave for another 2 to 4 minutes.

9. Carefully remove the potatoes from the microwave. **Cut** each potato lengthwise down the middle. Place each potato on a plate. Use spoons to **put** the beans, vegetables, cheese, and salsa on top. Each person can **fill** a potato with the toppings he or she likes.

TRY THIS!

Get creative with your toppings. Try sliced **olives**, **sour cream**, **cottage cheese**, **sunflower seeds**, **raisins**, grated **carrots**, or anything else you like. Yum!

Rolled-Up Lasagna

Try this fun twist on lasagna.
Each noodle is rolled up with goodies inside.

serves 6

preparation time: 25 minutes
baking time: 30 to 35 minutes

ingredients:
6 cups water
12 lasagna noodles
1 9-ounce package frozen spinach
2 cups cottage cheese or ricotta cheese
½ cup Parmesan cheese
¼ teaspoon salt
sprinkle of pepper
2 cups pasta sauce
4 ounces shredded mozzarella cheese

equipment:
liquid measuring cup
large saucepan with lid
wooden spoon
small microwave-safe bowl
oven mitts
colander
large bowl
measuring cups—½ cup, 1 cup
measuring spoons
spoon
9 x 9-inch baking pan
baking sheet

1. **Preheat** the oven to 350°F.

2. Measure 6 cups water and **pour** into a large saucepan. Place the saucepan on the stove and turn the burner under it to high. Cover the pan and heat until the water boils. **Add** the lasagna noodles. As they soften, use a wooden spoon to gently **push** them down under the water. Leave the cover off. Cook noodles for 12 to 14 minutes. (Or follow the directions on the lasagna package.)

Turn the page for more Rolled-Up Lasagna

3. While the noodles cook, prepare the other ingredients. **Open** the package of spinach and put it in a microwave-safe bowl. **Place** the bowl in the microwave for about 2 minutes, or until spinach is thawed. (Use oven mitts to take it out of the microwave, as the bowl might be hot.)

4. Place a colander in the sink. **Put** the spinach into the colander to **drain** off the liquid. If the spinach is hot, run cold water over it. Then **squeeze** the spinach with your clean hands to get the water out. Keep squeezing until no more liquid comes out.

5. In a large bowl, **add** spinach, cottage or ricotta cheese, Parmesan cheese, salt, and pepper. **Mix** the ingredients together with a spoon.

6. When the noodles are done cooking, have an adult **drain** them into a colander. Run the noodles under cold water.

7. **Spread** ½ cup pasta sauce in the bottom of a baking pan.

8. **Place** a cooked noodle on a baking sheet. **Spread** a thin layer of the cottage cheese mixture on the noodle (not too thick or it will be hard to roll). Start at one of the short sides of the noodle and **roll** it up. Carefully place the filled noodle in the pan. Make sure the seam of the rolled noodle is facing down. Repeat with each noodle until the pan is filled. The rolled noodles can be close together, but not touching.

9. **Pour** the rest of the pasta sauce over the noodles. **Sprinkle** the shredded mozzarella cheese over the top.

10. Use oven mitts to **place** the pan in the oven. **Bake** for 30 to 35 minutes, or until the cheese on top is melted and bubbly. **Remove** the pan with oven mitts. Serve.

TRY THIS!
This recipe doesn't have to be baked. Try eating the lasagna rolls cold. Just dip them in pasta sauce. You can even try packing a roll in your lunch!

serves 6 to 8

preparation time: 15 to 20 minutes
cooking time: 20 minutes

ingredients:

1 green pepper
1 medium onion
12 ounces firm tofu
1 6-ounce can tomato paste
1 14-ounce can diced tomatoes
2 teaspoons vegetable oil
½ cup water
1 teaspoon cumin
1 teaspoon oregano
1 teaspoon brown sugar
½ teaspoon salt
1 to 2 sprinkles of pepper
6 to 8 hamburger buns

equipment:

knife
cutting board
medium plate or bowl
fork
can opener
frying pan
measuring spoons
liquid measuring cup
wooden spoon

Who Needs Meat? Sloppy Joes

These delicious sloppy joes are made with a surprise ingredient—tofu. If you have never eaten tofu, this is a great dish to start with!

1. **Wash** the green pepper in cool water. Use the knife and cutting board to cut the vegetables. **Cut** around the stem of the green pepper. Then cut the green pepper in half and remove the seeds. Discard the stem and seeds. **Chop** enough of the rest of the green pepper to make 1 cup. Set aside.

2. **Cut** off both ends of the onion. Set the onion on one of the flat parts you made by cutting it. Cut the onion in half. **Peel** off and discard the papery layers around the outside. Lay the onion half flat on the cutting board. **Cut** the onion crosswise into semicircular slices. Then **chop** the slices into small pieces. Repeat with the other half. Set aside.

3. Put the tofu on a plate or in a bowl. **Mash** it into small chunks with a fork or with your hands.

4. Use a can opener to **open** the tomato paste. Then **open** the can of diced tomatoes. Do not pour out the juice.

5. Measure the oil and **pour** it in the frying pan. Turn the burner under the pan on medium. **Add** the onion and cook for 5 minutes, **stirring** with a wooden spoon. **Add** the green pepper and cook for 5 more minutes.

6. **Add** the tofu, tomato paste, diced tomatoes with their juice, and water. Then **add** cumin, oregano, brown sugar, salt, and a small sprinkle of pepper. **Stir** well with the wooden spoon. Turn the burner to low and simmer for 10 minutes.

7. **Serve** sloppy joe mix on hamburger buns.

serves 4 to 6

preparation time: 20 to 25 minutes
cooking time: 2 to 3 minutes

ingredients:

1 cup water
1 cup couscous
1½ cups garbanzo beans
1 tablespoon fresh basil leaves (or
    1 teaspoon dried)
⅓ cup raisins
¼ cup slivered almonds
1 lemon
¼ cup olive oil or vegetable oil
¼ teaspoon salt
1 to 2 sprinkles of pepper
1 orange

equipment:

liquid measuring cup
microwave-safe bowl
dinner plate
fork
can opener
colander
measuring spoons
large bowl
measuring cups—1 cup, ⅓ cup,
    ¼ cup
spoon
spatula
knife
cutting board
small bowl
grater

Lemony Couscous Salad

Have you ever cooked couscous? It's so quick and easy to make that it's kind of like magic. And this light and tasty salad will fill you right up.

1. Measure 1 cup of water in large microwave-safe bowl. **Place** in the microwave and cook until boiling. This will take 2 to 3 minutes, depending on your microwave.

2. When the water is boiling, ask an adult to take the bowl out of the microwave. Measure the couscous and **put** it in the boiling water. **Cover** with a dinner plate and let it sit for 5 minutes. After 5 minutes, **uncover** and **fluff** the couscous with a fork.

3. Use a can opener to **open** the garbanzo beans. Put a colander in the sink and **pour** the beans into the colander to drain the liquid.

4. **Tear** enough basil leaves into small pieces to make 1 tablespoon. Or use a measuring spoon to measure a teaspoon of dry basil.

5. Use a spatula to **put** the cooked couscous into a large bowl. **Add** raisins, almonds, garbanzo beans, and basil. **Mix** well with a spoon.

Turn the page for more Lemony Couscous Salad

6. Start the dressing for the salad. On a cutting board, **cut** the lemon in half. **Squeeze** half the lemon into a small bowl to get the juice out. You will need to **scoop** out the seeds with a small spoon. Repeat with the other half.

7. **Add** the oil, salt, and pepper to the lemon juice.

8. **Wash** the orange in cool water. Use a grater to **grate** the peel of the orange into the lemon juice dressing. Stop grating when you get to the orange's white layer. **Mix** the dressing well.

9. **Peel** the white skin off the orange. You may need an adult to help you cut off the skin with a knife. **Divide** the orange into sections. **Cut** the sections into smaller pieces using the knife and cutting board. **Add** the orange pieces to the large bowl of couscous and **mix**.

10. **Pour** the lemon dressing over the couscous salad. **Mix** with a spoon.

SPECIAL INGREDIENTS

basil: a leafy herb used to season food. You can often find fresh basil at the grocery store. Or if it's the right season, look for it at a farmers' market. Dried basil is located in the dried spice and herb section.

bay leaves: whole leaves used in soups and other recipes to give food flavor. Bay leaves are used whole, not cut into pieces. They aren't tasty to eat, so be sure to remove them from any dish before serving it. You can find bay leaves in the spice section of the grocery store.

bread crumbs: store-bought crumbs used for breaded foods. Bread crumbs often come in canisters and are sold in most grocery stores.

broth: the liquid part of a soup is called broth. Look in the soup section of a grocery store for broth. It comes in cans, cartons, and small jars. (Read the directions for use.)

cashews: curved nuts eaten roasted or used in Indian and Southeast Asian cooking

cilantro: an herb used to season food. You can often find fresh cilantro at the grocery store.

couscous: a grain often used in Middle Eastern cooking

cumin: the dried fruit of a plant in the parsley family used to flavor many Middle Eastern and Asian dishes. Look for ground cumin in the dried spice and herb section of your grocery store.

curry powder: a spice made from of a mix of Indian spices, including turmeric, cumin, ginger, coriander, and cloves. Look for curry in the spice aisle of the grocery store.

garbanzo beans: a type of legume, or bean, also called chickpeas. Look for them in the canned beans section.

ginger: a root used as a spice. You can find ground ginger in the spice section of the grocery store.

oregano: an herb used to season food. Dried oregano is located in the dried spice and herb section of a grocery store. Many grocery stores and farmers' markets have fresh oregano.

pita bread: round flatbread made with wheat flour that is typically served with Greek or Middle Eastern foods. Look for pita bread in the deli section of most grocery stores.

ricotta cheese: a thick, creamy cheese that comes in a tub and is commonly used in Italian foods. Look for ricotta cheese in the dairy section of your grocery store.

salsa: a sauce that may contain tomatoes, hot peppers, garlic, and herbs. It is often used to flavor Mexican dishes and can be found near the chips in the snack food aisle of the grocery store.

tofu: a food made from soybeans. Tofu is often kept in the produce section of a grocery store. Most Asian grocery stores also sell tofu.

FURTHER READING AND WEBSITES

ChooseMyPlate.gov
http://www.choosemyplate.gov/children
-over-five.html
Download coloring pages, play an
interactive computer game, and get
lots of nutrition information at this U.S.
Department of Agriculture website.

Farmers Markets Search
http://apps.ams.usda.gov/FarmersMarkets/
Visit this site to find a farmers' market
near you!

Gillies, Judi, and Jennifer Glossop. *The
Jumbo Vegetarian Cookbook*. Toronto: Kids
Can Press, 2002.
This book has even more vegetarian recipes
for kids.

Katzen, Mollie. *Honest Pretzels: And 64
Other Recipes for Cooks Ages 8 and Up*.

Berkeley, CA: Tricycle Press, 2009.
This cookbook includes a whole bunch of
vegetarian recipes.

Recipes
http://www.sproutonline.com/crafts-and-
recipes/recipes
Find more fun and easy recipes for kids at
this site.

Vegetarian Society
http://www.youngveggie.org/
Visit this website for kids to learn about
being a vegetarian.

LERNER _e_ SOURCE™

Expand learning beyond the printed
book. Download free, complementary
educational resources for this book from
our website, www.lerneresource.com.

INDEX